In the early days of autumn,
fruits and seeds ripen on the trees.
There is plenty for everyone to eat.

Now try this

Do you recognise these fruits and seeds?
Which ones can human beings eat?

4

5

But winter is coming.
Birds and animals need to eat plenty now.
Soon it will be hard to find food.
Some animals make a little store of
food for winter.

As the weather gets colder,
some animals find a
warm nest, burrow or cave
and go to sleep.

This is called hibernating.
They do not wake up
until the spring!

9

Some birds and animals move to warmer places when the weather gets colder.
Birds and insects may fly thousands of kilometres.
In the spring, they fly back again!

Try this later
Moving to another place is called migrating.
Find out which animals and birds are summer visitors to your area.

Some trees are evergreen.
They keep their leaves all winter.
But on many trees, the leaves begin to die.

Try this later
Autumn leaves turn beautiful colours.
Collect some of the prettiest ones.
Stick them on to card to make an autumn picture.

12

13

Autumn winds blow the leaves
from the trees.
Soon the branches are bare.

On autumn mornings,
it is sometimes misty.
It is hard to see very far ahead!

Sometimes a frost overnight
makes everything sparkle.

Gradually during the autumn,
the days become shorter.
It gets dark quite early in the evening.

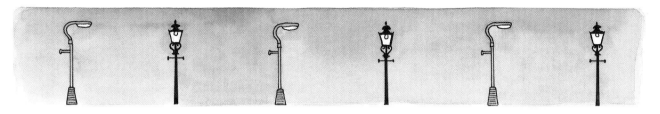

Try this later
On cold dark evenings, it is much warmer inside.
What do you do when you come home from school?

In the middle of autumn,
Halloween makes scary things fun.

Try this later
Ask a grown up to help you make
a scary face from autumn fruits.
Pumpkins are best.

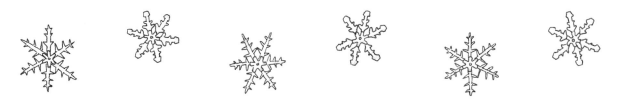

As the autumn passes, the days become colder and colder until... winter is here.

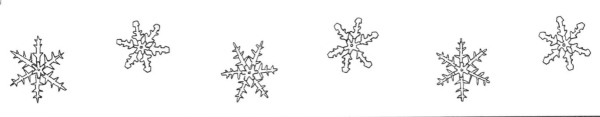

Index

This edition 2004
Franklin Watts
96 Leonard Street
London EC2A 4XD

Franklin Watts Australia
45-51 Huntley Street
Alexandria NSW 2015

Copyright © Franklin Watts 1996

Editor: Sarah Ridley
Designer: Kirstie Billingham
Picture researcher: Sarah Moule
ISBN: 0 7496 5226 8

A CIP catalogue record for this
book is available from the British
Library.

Dewey Decimal Classification
Number: 574.5

Acknowledgements:
The publishers would like to thank
Carol Olivier and Kenmont Primary
School for their help with the cover
of this book.

Photographs: Bruce Coleman Ltd 11;
James Davis Travel Photography 13;
Robert Harding Picture Library 14,
17; Peter Millard cover; NHPA 5, 7,
23; Oxford Scientific Films /
Animals Animals 9; TRIP 3;
ZEFA 16, 21.

Printed in Malaysia